LORD JE
CHRIST
Historicity and Millennium Hymn

by

Felix I.D. Konotey-Ahulu

LOXWOOD PRESS

First published 2023

Quotations from the Bible are
taken mainly from the Authorised Version

Material in chapter 1 on the Historicity and The Lord
Jesus Christ (Christmas) and chapter 2 on the Historicity of
The Lord Jesus Christ (Easter) first appeared in the
Ghanaian Times and is used by permission.
Material in chapter 3 was published in the British Medical Journal and is used by
permission.

Printed by Sussex Print Limited, Lancing, West Sussex
www.sussexprint.co.uk

Loxwood Press
50 Loxwood Avenue, Worthing, West Sussex BN14 7RA
Tel: 01903 232208

Contents

Preface

This book of four chapters contains two articles republished from The Ghanaian Times and one from The British Medical Journal with the kind permission of the editors, plus my MILLENNIUM HYMN in the last chapter. The main reason in producing them in book form is not only because they were greatly appreciated when first published in both Ghana and the United Kingdom, but also because they contain vital information that requires careful consideration by every reader. Christmas and Easter do not just become seasonal terms, but they undermine historical facts about The LORD JESUS CHRIST. In answering The British Medical Journal editor's question "Do you believe in God?" I used no less than 48 references to cover every considerable debating point that militant atheists threw at me in the various universities I have been fortunate to associate myself with, emphasizing the interaction of things like History, The Miraculous, and The Personal.

My Fourth Chapter "TIME WAS CREATED" is the hymn I wrote at the turn of The Millennium containing seven historical facts that define The LORD JESUS CHRIST. Whenever I sing The MILLENNIUM HYMN I stand erect on verse 7 as you can see on https://bit.ly/cRrZ0s (0 is zero, no o). May this book be a blessing to not a few!

FELIX I D KONOTEY-AHULU FGA MB BS MD(Lond) FRCP(Lond) FRCP(Glasg) DTMH(L'pool) DSc(Hon UCC) DSc(Hon UH) FGCP FWACP FTWAS ORDER OF THE VOLTA(Officer) – Kwegyir Aggrey Distinguished Professor of Human Genetics, University of Cape Coast, Ghana, and Former Consultant Physician Genetic Counsellor in Sickle Cell and Other Haemoglobinopathies, Korle Bu Teaching Hospital, Ghana, and Cromwell Hospital, London SW5 0TU, and 9 Harley Street Phoenix Hospital Group, London WIG 9AL [www.sicklecell.md]

Introduction

Professor Felix I. D. Konotey-Ahulu, a world authority on the sickle cell disease, the recipient of many awards, and a soldier for Africa in the medical world, would say that even more important is that he is a soldier of The Lord Jesus Christ.
In this short collection the reader sees that for Professor Konotey-Ahulu there should be no conflict between science and belief in God and The Lord Jesus Christ, and there are events which are "supra-scientific".
He shows that Christmas and Easter are far more than just seasonal festivals, but demonstrate that Christianity is based on proven historical facts and for the professor, History is important. He shares his personal testimony of why he believes in God. There is much that is thought provoking, even challenging, and ends with a triumphant Millennium hymn.

DONALD BANKS
Loxwood Press

The Three Wise Men looking for the Baby King of Kings

'The Christian faith … is based on a series
of historical events. It is an announcement
of events, historical happenings and of facts....
historical events connected with the life
and work and ministry, the death and resurrection
and ascension of the Son of God,
and with the descent of the Holy Ghost
on the Day of Pentecost.

Dr D. Martyn Lloyd-Jones
Exposition of chapters 3:20-4:25 of the Epistle to the Romans
BANNER OF TRUTH

1
Historicity of the Lord Jesus Christ (1)
Significance of Christmas

THE Lord Jesus Christ is the most attested fact in history. By dating a cheque December 17, 2022 before it can be cashed, the most adamant atheists acknowledge that, around two thousand and twenty-two years ago, a series of events began to happen, through which all world history has been dated for all time.

December 17, 2022 means December 17, 2022 AD, which means 2022 in the year ('Anno' in Latin) of The Lord (Domini). Which Lord are we talking about? Answer: The Lord Jesus Christ, because all time before His birth is 'BC' (Before Christ).

You see, whether the atheists like it or not, this is so. The Lord Jesus Christ has to be reckoned with. As promised several hundred years before it came to pass, Jesus, The Lord, was born miraculously. Supra-scientifically, in fact: "Behold, a virgin shall conceive, and bear a Son, and shall call his name Immanuel" (Isaiah chapter 7 verse 14). and it did happen.

Phenomena

Joseph was quite baffled by the angel telling him: "Do not be afraid to take to you Mary your wife, for that which is conceived in her is of the Holy Spirit" (Matthew chapter 1 verse 20). "And she will bring forth a Son, and you shall call His name JESUS, for He will save His people from their sins."

The historical account goes on: "Now all this was done, that it might be fulfilled which was spoken by the Lord through the prophet, saying 'Behold, the virgin shall be with child, and bear a Son, and they shall call his name Immanuel', which is translated, "God with us"'. (Matthew chapter 1 verses 22 & 23).

And this would happen at a geographically pinpointed place exactly as prophesied centuries before: "But you, Bethlehem Ephratah, though you are little among the thousands of Judah, yet out of you shall he come forth to Me, The One to be Ruler in Israel, Whose goings forth are from of old, from everlasting" (Micah chapter 5 verse 2). Mary had to trek from Nazareth to Bethlehem with Joseph because Caesar Augustus, the then Roman Emperor, had decreed that "all the world should be registered...So all went to be registered, everyone to his own city" (Luke chapter 2 verses 1-3).

On arrival in Bethlehem, Mary promptly went into labour. All the hotels were full, so she gave birth in a stable, with the animals looking on. The rest is history.

Angels, jubilant, alerted shepherds that the newborn baby was no ordinary baby. Wise men trekked from afar to see this baby. King Herod was furious when the wise men asked him where "the king" was born. Herod called the professors with much learning and asked them where it was stated in the sacred writings that a rare king would be born.

Bethlehem, of course, so Herod asked the wise men to go and find the baby, and report back so that he would also go and worship him. Liar! He wanted to kill The Lord Jesus, and the angels knew this, so they warned the wise men not to go back to Herod. The crafty old fox waited, and waited, but no wise men came back, so he embarked on widespread slaughter of children.

Listen to Matthew in chapter 2 verse 16: "Then Herod, when he saw that he was deceived by the wise men, was exceedingly angry, and he sent forth and put to death all the male children who were in Bethlehem and in all the districts, from two years old and under, according to the time that he had determined from the wise men."

The baby Lord Jesus would have been among the slaughtered children had not the angel of the Lord warned Joseph: "Arise, take the young Child and His mother, flee to Egypt, and stay there until I bring you word: for Herod will seek the young Child to destroy Him." (Matthew chapter 2 verse 13)

Just a few words here about this historical detail: When people tell me that I should have nothing to do with Christianity because it is a European religion, I take it upon myself to educate them.

First, I tell them The Lord Jesus learned to walk, not on the continent of Europe, but in Mizraim (Egypt), in Africa. Secondly, when the Ethiopian eunuch, Chancellor of the Exchequer of Queen Candace, became a Christian while reading the prophet Isaiah chapter 53, and Phillip helped him to understand what he was reading, the natives of the British Isles were only just in the process of being educated by the Romans to read and write.

So let nobody tell you that the Gospel of The Lord Jesus Christ is a European invention.

Science

Now, to sum up this extraordinary history so far: Virgin Birth, Bethlehem. Angels. Wise men led by a guiding star that stood just above where the baby was. Warning about Herod's wickedness. Fleeing to Mizraim. These things are supra-scientific (above science) because the phenomena involved are too deep for science to unravel.

I have read Medicine, and I can tell you there is no mention of "saving people from sin" in any textbook. Science cannot explain spiritual beings like angels. Science has no vocabulary for the spiritual. Virgin birth was ordered to happen, and it did happen.

Why is Science so useless in spiritual things? Answer: Because science is limited. What was told the Virgin Mary is out of bounds to Science: "The Holy Ghost shall come upon you, and the power of the Highest shall overshadow you; therefore also the Holy One who is to be born will be called the Son of God." (Luke chapter 1 verse 35)

Amazing! Many a scientific atheist, or atheistic scientist, has tried to wrap their brains around this phenomenon, and failed. There simply is no scientific meaning to this. We can certainly rely on Science to help us fly an aeroplane, speak to people 10,000 miles away, land on the moon, analyse the rings around the planet Saturn, but we cannot rely on Science to help us know God, know His character, know His plan for the world and our place in it, nor know the meaning of 'eternal life'. In the realm of life after death, Science is useless. Totally.

Science has its uses, but in the things that really matter in life, we must look elsewhere.

Where then do we find answers to questions of eternal dimension? Answer: History. To me, history is the most important subject in the world. This is why atheists are for ever trying to rewrite it. The latest attempt is by one Dan Brown who would dearly want to wish away the facts of 'AD' and 'BC'. He will fail, as many before him have done.

To me, the words of The Lord Jesus Christ in His prayer to God The Father, recorded in John chapter 17, especially verse 3, are so astonishing as to take my breath away: "And this is life eternal, that they may know You, the only true God, and Jesus Christ whom You have sent."

I have underlined this in my Bible, for there is something called eternal life. There is something called knowing God, "The only True God". And there is the fact of Jesus Christ (AD and BC), whom God The Father has sent. But why has God sent Him? Answer: That we might know God, whom to know is life eternal.

What does this mean? To ask you to read the entire Bible from Genesis to Revelation in order to find the answer to this question is too huge a task, so why not try just one of the 66 books of the Bible to start with – like the Gospel of John, and go through it? You will not understand everything, but you will understand enough to set you well on the way to knowing God, The Only True God, and Jesus Christ whom He has sent. Will you take up the challenge?

A few tips

You will observe that this word "sent" mentioned in the verse above (John chapter 17 verse 3) is the 34th time The Lord Jesus said He was sent. I commend this exercise to you. Count how often He said He was "sent". Forty times! Yes, 40 times in the Gospel of John alone.

When I discovered this as I read through the entire book of John, I became frightened. Really, I was frightened. Because the question that arose in my mind was this: "What have I done in my life, with God's Messenger, The Lord Jesus Christ?"

Most readers of this booklet are less than half my age. You need to ask yourself that question too: What have you done in life with the One whom God has sent? Why did God send Him? The Apostle John tells us the answer to that question too.

The Lord Jesus is The Creator of the world. This Baby? Yes, the Baby! John chapter 1 verses 1-5, especially verse 3: "All things were made through Him, and without Him was not anything made that was made." The world, you see, is no cosmic accident. This world was created by The Triune GOD, and through this Lord Jesus, who was born in Bethlehem.

So why did He have to be born? Answer: The world God created was perfect, flawless, and sinless. Adam and Eve knew God intimately in the Garden of Eden. But then came The Fall, when God's arch enemy, the Devil, Satan, Lucifer, the Deceiver, deceived our spiritual representatives, Adam and Eve, who were then thrown out of Paradise and lost the knowledge of God and forfeited communion with The Creator.

"Oh, but Dr Konotey-Ahulu," I hear you object, "this is Sunday School stuff. Do you still believe this nonsense?" ANSWER: This is no nonsense. I most certainly have come back to believing this history of mankind, after disputing it briefly when reading science in university.

I tell you, nothing makes sense of life as I know it: wars, rumours of wars, strife (domestic and international), earthquakes and volcanoes, wickedness, injustice, sin and its consequences, pain and suffering, disease (hereditary and acquired).

Saviour

Nothing, but nothing, makes sense to me until I see it through the history of Perfect Creation, the Fall and its terrible consequences, the Promise of God, not only to undo the damage Satan has wrought, but also to restore man's communion with Himself through His Son who would become Incarnate (GOD becoming Man) by being "sent into the world", and who (unlike Adam and Eve) would pay perfect obedience to God's laws, and would, by supra-scientific deeds on earth, prove that He was no ordinary person.

He would satisfy the full justice of God (which Adam and Eve could not do), and pay the eternal punishment for sins, so that those offspring of rebellious Adam who believe on Him would not perish, but have eternal life. "For God so loved the world that He gave His only begotten Son, that whoever believes in Him should not perish, but have everlasting life" (John chapter 3 verse 16).

Finally, if I did not believe this, I would find it impossible to give a satisfactory explanation for life after death. Indeed, the Apostle James tells us that the devils believe this and tremble because they know that there is no salvation for them (See James chapter 2 verse 19). These fallen angels, unlike humans, cannot repent.

Fortunately, for me, I can repent and believe on this Saviour who loved me and gave Himself for me so that I can have communion restored with my Creator, who became flesh, paid my penalty at Golgotha, was dead and buried, and rose again with power on the third day, to prove that GOD did indeed accept His substitutionary atonement for me.

"Oh, come, come, Dr Konotey-Ahulu," says someone, "all this is too difficult for me to understand."

Of course it is! I myself do not understand it either – how God can become flesh, and how God can die, and on the third day rise again with power – I do not, I cannot take it all in. But I do believe it, and that is all that matters.

Remember Thomas? I mean scientific Thomas, regarding the resurrection of the Lord Jesus Christ? True scientist that he was, he wanted Evidence: not only visual evidence ("Unless I see in His hands the print of the nails"), but also tactile evidence ("and put my finger into the print of the nails, and put my hand into His side"), I will not believe." (John chapter 20 verse 25).

And you remember how The Blessed Risen Lord Jesus replied (verse 27) when He reappeared to the disciples? "Peace to you." Then He said to Thomas, "Reach out your finger here, and look at My hands: and reach your hand here, and put it into My side. Do not be unbelieving, but believing."

Flabbergasted, Thomas could only say: "My Lord and my God!" And listen to The Lord's response in verse 29: "Thomas, because you have seen me, you have believed. Blessed are those who have not seen and yet have believed."

So, dear reader, do not try to understand the suprascientific. Do not try to understand The Lord Jesus Christ. Just seek Him, and believe Him. As wise men of old travelled from afar to seek Him, found Him, and worshipped Him, so wise men and women today seek Him, find Him, and worship Him. Are you one of them?

If you are, please join me to sing my Millennium hymn, which was first sung by the choir of the University of Cape Coast, and later by Achimota School Choir. The melody that I composed to go with it is called "All Time Pre and Post 2000AD", beautifully harmonised by my sister, Edna Soyannwo.

The entire hymn is on page 28, complete with Tonic Solfa. Please seek Him, find Him, and worship Him. The first verse of my Millennium Hymn goes:

Time was created and initiated by Him;
Present time, is maintained accurately by Him;
Future time wll be commanded and held by Him
Who, though God, became Incarnate at Bethlehem.

Empty grave: the stone rolled away

Historicity of The Lord Jesus Christ (2)
Significance of Easter

THAT I am a sinner I have no doubt. That there are voices out there that are competing with each other to convince me otherwise is also not in doubt. These voices, or views, which assert themselves daily, insist I am wrong to think of myself as a sinner.

I can enumerate 10 of these views, but there are more. I may not be as bad as some people, says one view, but to say I am a sinner is going too far. Another view says there is no such thing as sin, and I need to abandon such medieval concepts and get back into the 21st Century.

A **third view** (some call it the scientific view) is that the universe, and my place in it, is a cosmic accident (Big Bang and all that), and to begin talking about sin is sheer fantasy and a waste of time.

A **fourth view** disagreeing with me, says that to call myself a sinner is clear evidence that I have succumbed to missionary indoctrination aimed at making me so docile as to enable imperialists to come and steal my land, timber, minerals, especially gold.

A **fifth view** urges that the less we hear about 'sin' and 'sinner' and 'Christianity', the better, because it was Christian countries that took human cargo as slaves across the Atlantic.

A **sixth view**, Africo-centric, points out that Africans already have a rich heritage of religious experience and do not need foreigners to tell them whom and what to worship.

A **seventh view**, currently articulated from the University of Manchester, says church attendance in the UK is diminishing so fast that there will be no Church by the end of this Century, so what am I fussing about sin for?

An **eighth view** says Christianity is nothing more than a money making business, so all this talk of 'sin' is just a means to an end, the end being getting very rich by persuading people to flock in to get their diseases healed, and send in their tithes without fail.

The **nineth view** is a psychological attack. It warns about losing my self esteem when I refer to myself as a sinner. Get rid of this idea of sin, shouts this voice, and build up your self- esteem by positive thinking.

I could go on and on, but the **tenth attack** on my "I'm a sinner" position has a pseudo-intellectual appeal because its ammunition is, deliberately, marshalled against the real answer to the above-mentioned views.

History is the most important weapon fighting alongside truth, hence in his best seller *"The Da Vinci Code"*, Dan Brown sets out deliberately to rewrite the **historicity of the Lord Jesus Christ**. With all his 'hard work' (for which incidentally, he has recently been taken to court for allegedly reproducing somebody else's earlier 'hard work'), Dan Brown has not succeeded in changing 'BC' *(Before Christ)* or today's date in 2023 AD to something else. Why? Because BC is truth, and so is AD *(Anno Domini* – in the year of Our Lord.

This is how I put it in my first chapter on The Historicity of The Lord Jesus: "To me history is the most important subject in the world. This is why atheists are for ever trying to rewrite it."

In this second chapter I give an explanation of important dates in the Christian Calendar – **Christmas** (the miraculous, indeed supra-scientific birth of **The Lord Jesus Christ**) and **Easter** (the murder of **The Lord Jesus**, and His, again supra-scientific, bodily resurrection – events whose explanation scientists cannot wrap around their brains.

Good Friday

So if Jesus (I prefer to call Him The Lord Jesus) was murdered without having committed any crime, why do I call the day we remember 'GOOD FRIDAY' and not Bad Friday?

ANSWER: Because the One who made the Diagnosis of 'Sin' in me (and I thoroughly agree with that Diagnosis), and whose Treatment for 'Sin' is so radical and so drastic, as to have meant my total banishment out of His sight, and punishment for this 'Sin', is the same One [GOD ALMIGHTY] who, for some inscrutable reason, loved me so much that He transferred (yes, I mean transferred) my transgression upon His sinless Son, dealing with Him as if it were He who transgressed, and made Him pay the price for 'Sin', so that I could go scot-free.

Please read that again because it is mind-boggling. Indeed, the Jews found the teaching a stumbling block to faith, and as for the intellectuals, the Greeks, they thought what I have just said about Jesus being punished for someone's sin, sheer nonsense.

This is how the Apostle Paul put it in 1 Corinthians chapter 1 verses 22 & 23: "Jews demand miraculous signs and Greeks look for wisdom, but **we preach Christ crucified**: a stumbling block to Jews and to the Greeks foolishness".

Then the thing that really makes me rejoice in Good Friday is what I call **the reverse transfer of righteousness** to me the sinner.

Not only are my filthy rags of Sin placed on The Lord Jesus Christ and punished on Him (as Isaiah prophesied long ago in Chapter 53 – please read it), but The Lord's beautiful **robe of righteousness** is transferred to me the moment I believe on Him.

The **Ga** language puts Count Zinzendorf's hymn wonderfully: *"Mitade ke miwole fee, dzi Kristo la ke dzale le"*, meaning *"Jesus, Thy blood and righteousness my beauty are, my glorious dress"* which makes GOD see me (the rogue) as if I have never sinned. Amazing transaction, that! Apostle Paul renders it like this: **"For God**

hath made Him (The Lord Jesus Christ) who knew no sin, to be sin for us that we might be made the righteousness of God in Him."

Some modern theologians think they are cleverer than God and say things like: The Lord Jesus it was who begged God to forgive us for killing Him and that 14 April should really be called 'Bad Friday'.

No, says Scripture. "Jesus of Nazareth, a man approved of God among you by miracles and wonders and signs, which God did by him in the midst of you, as you yourselves also know; " [Apostle Peter continues] Him, being delivered by the determinate counsel and foreknowledge of God, you have taken, and by wicked hands have crucified and slain."

Do you get that? What the murderers did was diabolical, but it was God who determined that, and abandoned His eternal Son as punishment for my sin. No wonder the holy angels were completely baffled (according to Apostle Peter) about how God, who hates sin, set about the problem of punishing sin while justifying the sinner. This is called **GRACE** – defined as *'Favour shown to the undeserving sinner'*. **JUSTICE** is the *'Deserved consequence of, or punishment for sin'*.

MERCY is 'Withholding deserved punishment'. We see all three at *Golgotha*. Justice was done there. Sin was comprehensively dealt with, so that God who hates sin was vindicated, when He forsook His Son because of Sin, howbeit the Sin of others. Mercy too was much in evidence, when the punishment I deserved was not meted to me.

And, surprise, surprise, the robe of righteousness I do NOT deserve, is given to me on the merits of my blessed Saviour. That was Grace. To show that God approved of the transaction, He raised The Lord Jesus from the dead. Proof that all this was planned is in the fact that The Lord Jesus, as I point out in the earlier chapter, said no less than 40 times in the Gospel of the Apostle John that He, The Son, was *"sent"* into the world for just this purpose: to reconcile believers to God the Father.

Don't take it from me, read it yourself and count the number of times the word *"sent"* comes out of the mouth of The Saviour. If, as Dan Brown would have us believe, The Lord Jesus was not Who He said He was, then He lied no less than 40 times! Make up your own mind. Now listen to three True Stories.

True Story Number 1

John Newton (1725-1807), married man, a professed Christian, and captain of a Slave ship, had the use of a concubine in Accra whenever he visited the west coast of Africa to collect slaves across the Atlantic. He threw those who were sick overboard to perish in the sea. Very wicked, he was.

But then John Newton was convicted of sin. He heard this Good News that though GOD hated his sin, He loved the sinner (John chapter 3, verses 14 to l6). Do please read these verses.

Newton repented, understood the meaning of Grace, and wrote this hymn:

"Amazing grace! How sweet the sound,
that saved a wretch like me!
I once was lost, but now am found;
was blind, but now I see."

True story Number 2

Felix Konotey-Ahulu was a Foundation Member at Legon Hall, where he had succeeded Mr Adade as General Secretary of the SCM (Students' Christian Movement). Felix "was born a Christian" because his father was 'Basel Presby Osofo'. Baptised and confirmed, Domeno thought if anyone could be called a Christian, he must be the one. He played the piano, and was in the University Church Choir, with the best of them.

One auspicious evening, alone in his room at **8pm, Friday 24th October 1952**, reading the day's Scripture portion in the Gospel of Matthew, which said The Lord Jesus did not come to call the righteous but sinners to repentance, I [Domeno] was stung! Surely, HE did not come tor me, because I [Felix] was not a sinner; certainly not as bad as So-and-so, or So-and-so, or So-and-so.

I began to beg that HE should come for me, "because I now realise that I am a sinner, worse than So-and-so, or So-and-so....". Before then, I would be asking people to define sin, and would sound very clever debating what could be called sin, and what not.

Suddenly, I realised sin was not difficult to define. It was living as if God did not exist. Living for self. I was the greatest hypocrite on the Legon campus. I spare you the details, but I got up, tears in my eyes, went next door, knocked on the door of James Mustaffah, and told him: "Felix will not be the same again." I was never the same again.

Soon I realised that those who have been forgiven much, love to live lives pleasing to God. That was how I recognised a few English couples in Accra who were totally different from all the other white people I knew. Ralph Hulme, my Chemistry teacher (and his wife Shelagh), Honor Ward my Physics teacher (and her husband Professor Alan Ward), and Tony Wilmot, later Kwame Nkrumah's Senior Principal Secretary, Communications (and his wife Eve).

True Story Number 3

Brian Williams was a couple of years behind me in Westminster Hospital Medical School, London University. Like the majority of British students he despised going to church. I loved going to hear Dr Martyn Lloyd-Jones, previously a Cardiologist at St Bartholomew's Hospital, but who now preached powerful sermons at Westminster Chapel, near Buckingham Palace.

Brian and I would often stay up late at our hostel, debating everything under the sun, including religion. At last, Brian agreed to come to church with me. That Sunday night Dr Lloyd-Jones preached on Golgotha, and what was really happening there.

As we walked to the hospital after the service, I dared not ask Brian how he felt, or even say a word lest I detracted from the awesome message we had just heard.

We walked along Victoria Street and Vauxhall Bridge Road in complete silence, until just as we entered Brabazon House Brian said to me: "Felix, Dr Lloyd-Jones said all that needed to be done for my Salvation has been done. Is it true?" Yes, I said.

As the third verse of the last hymn ('O happy day that fixed my choice') puts it:

'Tis done! The great transaction's done!
I am my Lord's and He is mine;
He drew me and I followed on,
Charmed to confess the voice divine.'
[Phillip Doddridge, 1702-51]

Brian said, "Come into my room, Felix." We knelt down, and Brian gave himself to The Lord Jesus Christ. He was never the same again. He went on to become Professor of Epidemiological Medicine in the Universities of Sheffield and Nottingham. I received a letter from Brian at Christmas 2004 thanking me profusely for taking him to hear Dr Martyn Lloyd-Jones in 1957. He said he was ill with a rare muscle disease.

Five months later, one morning, while in bed, Brian called his wife Catherine and asked for a particular tape-recorded sermon of Dr Martyn Lloyd-Jones. While listening to it, Brian Williams passed from time into eternity.

Is Easter significant in the 22nd Century? Ten voices and views will ask you to forget that The Lord Jesus said 40 times He was sent specifically to die on the Cross, and to rise again on the third day. This Saviour does not lie. When He says He will come again, He surely will.

These chapters first appeared as articles in The Ghanaian Times on Saturday, December 17, 2005, and on Saturday, April 8, 2006 and have been updated.

Personal Answer to the Question "DO YOU BELIEVE IN GOD?"

https://www.bmj.com/content/319/7214/929.2/rr-0

MENTIONING God four times in headlines June to December 2017 [1-4] the BMJ is clearly not scared of ridicule from the author of *"The God Delusion"* and *"The Greatest Show on Earth: the evidence for evolution"* Richard Dawkins [5,6]. Numerous publications demolish the "scientific" foundation of his militant atheism [7-22]. Reading Professor David Berlinski's excellent book *"The Devil's Delusion: Atheism and its Scientific Pretensions"* [23] I discern a vast difference between his Princeton PhD-reasoning and Dawkin's Oxford University D.Phil-cogitations. Thankfully, Oxford University has at least three other D.Phils who believe in the GOD Dawkins denies. Dr Jim Packer's *"Knowing God"* is a gem of a Classic [24]; Professor John Lennox outshines Professor Richard Dawkins [25 26] in Public Debates, and Dawkins' previous fellow atheist Professor Alister McGrath writes: "There are many who are deluded about God, and I used to be one of them." [27]. His bestseller *"The Dawkins Delusion? Atheist fundamentalism and the denial of the divine"* [27] states (page 64), "The God delusion is a work of theatre, rather than scholarship..." Alister McGrath and his wife Joanna Collicutt McGraph conclude their book with this question: "Might atheism be a delusion about God?" [27]

To whom is this question directed? [1]

The "you" of Modern English is ambiguously singular and plural. I prefer "thou" and "ye" of yesteryears, and I split the question into "Dost thou acknowledge God's existence?" and "Dost thou believe in God?" Answering "Yes!" to both, I rest my confidence on three supra-scientific Facts: History, Miracle (properly defined) and Personal Experience.

History

Historical events that cannot be fathomed through Science are often either dismissed as myths (never happened) or explained away somehow. Professor Know-All's comments in the BMJ on four historical events in Clinical Medicine that I called "supra-scientific" proves my point. [28] The fourth event I described was when my robust younger brother announced on Friday 16th December one year that he had a week to live, and the following Wednesday 21st December, as our mother was baking cakes for Christmas, he said none of us would be eating cakes that Christmas and we laughed him to scorn; then playing football with him on Friday 23rd December we were both struck by lightning which killed him instantly, and left me with a facial burn. [29] Not only did Jerry have "a week to live", but also no one ate cakes at Christmas 1949 in Odumase-Krobo while Rev. D.A. Konotey-Ahulu's second son lay unburied on Christmas Day. Professor Know-All's "scientific" verdict was, "Your brother was accident prone"! [30]

Moses saw the burning bush that was not consumed and, advancing to investigate, heard, "Moses, Moses! Draw not nigh hither. Put off thy shoes from off thy feet, for the place whereon thou standest is holy ground." He was petrified when the voice said "I AM. THAT I AM .. Thus shalt thou say unto the children of Israel 'I AM hath sent me unto you.'" [31] Truth of this historical event baffles atheists. That Moses went on to deliver his people from slavery in Egypt is sheer history. [32]

When I date my cheques 20th January 2023 I am proclaiming that 20 centuries ago The Lord Jesus Christ said in Jerusalem, "Before Abraham was I AM', [33] the very name that Moses heard at the burning bush. I do not appeal to Science for help in validating the historicity of The Lord Jesus Christ who said 40 times in Apostle John's Gospel that He was sent. [34] His origins and deeds can only be described as miraculous.

What is a miracle?

December 1958 to March 1959 was a bad winter for this African in London. Weeks before Final Exams in April 1959 to graduate as a doctor I was admitted with virus pneumonia to Westminster Hospital in Horseferry Road under Dr (later) Sir Richard Bayliss, Queen's Physician. If I recovered there was no way I could pass the exam because my revision plans were ruined. Discharged in time to sit the Finals, I passed.

My friend Richard Alderson, brilliant English Teacher, and fellow member of Dr Martyn Lloyd-Jones' Westminster Chapel [35], later saw me and asked how I did. His immediate response when I said, " I passed. It's a miracle!" taught me the correct meaning of the word: "If you had the brain of a hedgehog that would be a miracle." Exactly! True miracles are way beyond the merely supra-scientific. The hedgehog-brain-answering-exam-questions-on-placenta-praevia type of historical event that defies scientific explanation, is what some scientists deny ever happened. But Nobel Prize winner Sir Peter Medawar published *"The Limits of Science."* [36] Lesser-brained scientists disagree, claiming (like Professor Know-All) to have answers for everything.

Well then, "Crucified, dead, and buried; the third day The Lord Jesus rose from the dead" is not Science so is it not History either? Does History not confirm mysterious truths which Science cannot fathom? [37, 38] I knew some Resurrection deniers who hated The Lord Jesus Christ. Their "OK, Jesus rose from the dead, so what?" reveals much. Are they God haters rather than just atheists? Are we really in a "Post-Truth World"? [39]

Personal Experience

"GOD is a SPIRIT, and they that worship Him must worship Him in spirit and in truth" [40] – words of The Lord Jesus Christ once quite meaningless to me. Science had/has no definition for "spiritual things" [41-43]. But on Friday 24 October 1952, alone in my university rooms in Ghana reading other words of The Lord Jesus [44] He mirculously revealed Himself to me. There's no scientific explanation for what happened that night. Subdued and tearful, I went next-door to tell fellow student James Mustaffah: "Felix will never be the same again!" [45]. I was never the same again. Similar experiences described in Eric Metaxas's remarkable biographies of Bonhoeffer, Wilberforce, and Luther [46-48] demonstrate this divine intertwining of History, Miracle, and Personal Experience. For me to understand spiritual things now is a Miracle. O Thank GOD!

Competing interest: Believer in The Lord Jesus Christ [Nuntsɔ Yesu Kristo]
felix@konotey-ahulu.com Twitter@profkonoteyahul

1 Saripanidis Savros. Do you believe in God? 24 August 2017 BMJ Rapid Response http://www.bmj.com/content/359/bmj.j4669/rapid-resonses Re Kevin Barraclough Do you believe in God?

2 Burridge Stan. Three forms of identification and a letter from God. BMJ 25 October 2017. 359: j4669. Doi: 10.1136/bmj.j4669 pmid: 29070597.

3 Donne J. 'Hymn to God, in My Sickness' ‖ BMJ Supportive & Palliative spcare. bmj.com/content/bmjspcare/7/3/273.full.pdf June 27 2017
John Donne's sonnet 'Death be not proud' is a favourite reading at funerals, but his 'Hymn to God, My God, in My Sickness' is one of the greatest poems in the language.

4 Keown Daniel. 'What God forgot to tell surgeons: the science of acupuncture'. Review by Anne-Marie Marlow. Downloaded on December 8 2017. http://aim.bmj.com/content/acupmed/31/3/3445.full.pdf

5 Dawkins Richard. 'The God Delusions'. London – Transworld Publications 2007.

6 Dawkins Richard. 'The Greatest Show on Earth'. Free Press, New York, 2009.

7 Sarfati Jonathan. 'The Greatest Hoax On Earth?' Refuting Dawkins On Evolution. Creation Book Publishers, Atlanta Georgia, USA, 2010. ISBN 978-0-949906-73-1 [333 pages]

8 'Evolution's Achilles Heels' – 9 PhD Scientists explain evolution's fatal flaws – in areas claimed to be its greatest strengths. Foreword by Carl Wieland. Creation Book Publishers, Powder Springs, Georgia, USA 2014. ISBN 978-1-921643-82-8 [272 pages]

9 Sarfati Jonathan. 'Refuting Evolution'. Amazon.com: Books 9780949906731 http//www.amazon.com/Refuting.Evolution-Jonathan-Sarfati/dp/0949906735 [A handbook for students, parents, and teachers countering the latest arguments for evolution]

10 Sarfati Jonathan. 'Refuting Evolution 2'. A sequel that comprehensively counters arguments that support evolution (as presented in TV Documentaries and Scientific American) 2004 ISBN 0-949906-27-1 [236 pages] www.amazon.co.uk/refuting+evolution+2

11 Penner JG. 'Evolution Challenged by Language and Speech'. Minerva Press, London W173YP. 2000 ISBN 0-75411-092-3 [403 pages]

12 Gitt Werner. 'In the beginning was information – A Scientist Explains the Incredible Design in Nature'. Master Books. New Leaf Publishing Group. AR 72638 USA. ISBN 13: 978-0-89051-461-0 & 10: 089051-461-5 [264 pages]

13 Gitt Werner. 'Did God use Evolution?' Christliche Literatur-Verbreitung e. V. Postfach 11 01-35-33661 Bielefeld Germany 2nd Edition 2001 [160 pages]

14 Sanford JC. 'Genetic Entropy'. FMS Publications (FMS Foundation) USA. Fourth Edition 2014. ISBN 978-0-9816316-0-8 [271 pages]

15 Wieland Carl. 'One Human Family. The Bible, Science, Race & Culture'. Creation Book Publihers, Stlanta, Georgia, USA 2011 [378 pages] www.one humanfamily.us

16 Andrews Edgar. 'Who Made GOD? Searching for a Theory of Everything'. EP Books, Pistyll, Pistyll, Holywell, CH8 7SH [324 pages] www.epbooks.org

17 Rendle-Short John. 'Green Eyes of the Storm. Controversy between Science and Christianity in the lives of Arthur Rendle-Short (1880-1953); Philip Henry Gosse (1810-1888); George John Romanes (1848-1894)'. The Banner of Truth Trust, Edinburgh/Pennsylvania 1998. ISBN 0-85151-7277 [294 pages]

18 Hoyle Fred. 'The Intelligent Universe'. Michael Joseph, London, 1985, page 25 "Why has the Darwinian theory of evolution by natural selection managed for upwards of a century to fasten itself like a superstition on so-called enlightened opinion? Why is the story still defended so vigorously?" [This from a Cambridge University Professor & a Fellow of UK's prestigious Royal Society FRS]

19 Sarfati Jonathan. 'By Design – Evidence for Nature's Intelligent Designer – The God of the Bible'. Creation Book Publishers 2008 Atlanta, Georgia, USA. [260 pages]
www.creationbookpublishers.com

20 Konotey-Ahulu FID. The God Delusion titles devalues sensible discourse. BMJ Rapid Response. October 19 2016.
www.bmj.com/content/335/7629/1099.1/rr-0

21 Blanchard John. 'Does GOD believe in Atheists?' Evangelical Press 2001, USA PO Box 84, Aubum, MA. 01501, USA ISBN 0-85234-460-0 [656 pages]

22 Blanchard John. 'Is GOD past His Sell-By Date?' Evangelical Press 2007. PO Box 825, Webster, NY 14580 & Faverdale North Industrial Estate, Darlington DL3 0PH, England. [268 pages]

23 Berlinski David. 'The Devil's Delusion: Atheism and its Scientific Pretension'. Basic Books (Perseus Books Group) 2009, 387 Park Avenue South, New York, NY 10016-8810. ISBN 978-0-465-01937-3

24 Packer J. 'Knowing God'. Hodder and Stoughton, London 1973 [256 pages]

25 Has Science buried God? Dr Richard Dawkins vs Dr John Lennox. YouTube Larry Alex Tauton 1 June 2017 [1 Hour 21 Minutes 53 Seconds]

26 The God Delusion Debate. Richard Dawkins and John Lennox. YouTube Larry Alex Tauton 29 January 2010 [1 Hour 3 Minutes]

27 McGrath Alister with McGraph JC. 'The Dawkins Delusion? Atheist Fundamentalism and the denial of the divine'. SPCK, 36 Causion Street, London SW19 4ST. 2007. ISBN 978-0-281-05927-0.

28 Konotey-Ahulu FID. The supra-scientific in clinical medicine: a challenge to Professor Know-All.
Doi:10.1136bmj.323.7327.1452 Brit Med J 2001; 323(7327); 1452-1453 (22-29 Dec)
http://www.bmj.com/cgi/reprint/323/7327/1452.pdf

29 Konotey-Ahulu FID. Case of lightning burns. BMJ 1963; 1:1547. June 8.
Doi. 1136/bmj.1.5344.1547
ncbi.nim.nih.gov/pmc/articles/PMC/2422124183/?pages=1

30 Konotey-Ahulu FID. Superstition and phenomena in Africa. Personal View. BMJ 1969; 2:48. April 15 doi:10.1136/bmj.2.5648.48
http://www.bmj.com/cgi/reprint/3/5664/235.pdf

31 Holy Bible: Exodus chapter 3 verses 1-10. [Moses commissioned to go ahead and lead Israelites out of Egypt].

32 Holy Bible: The Passover. Exodus chapter 12 verses 1 to 51. [Verse 51 "And it came to pass, … that The LORD brought the children of Israel out of the land of Egypt according to their armies" [A supra-scientific historical event]

33 LORD JESUS CHRIST. "Most assuredly, I say unto you, before Abraham was I AM." Gospel of John chapter 8 verse 58.

34 Konotey-Ahulu FID. MILLENNIUM Hymn – TIME WAS CREATED (Verse 3 of the 7 verses emphasises 40 times The LORD JESUS said in the Gospel of John that He was sent into the world and why – http://bit.ly/cRrZ0s (0 is zero, not o) 2000 Video with music http://www.youtube.com/watch?v=4hconD91uNs

35 Murray Ian. 'Life of Martyn Lloyd-Jones 1899-1980.' Banner of Truth Trust, Edinburgh [See Reference 24 of http://bit.ly/2igdDg2 for more details on him]

36 Medawar Peter. 'The Limits of Science'. Oxford University Press. 1985.

37 Konotey-Ahulu FID. 'History versus Limits of Science: Is Solomonic Genius a Y Chromosome Phenomenon?' J Genet Disorders Genetic Reports 2014; 3:2 http://bit.ly/1wyg5//H5

38 Konotey-Ahulu FID. 'Private Thoughts: There is no evidence that I was born on a Saturday'. Postgraduate Medical Journal of Ghana 1:32-33" [which often proved the superiority of history over science arriving at truth] 2012.

39 Konotey-Ahulu FID. Evidence in a post-truth world: Scientists' Misinformation and Disinformation https://bit.ly/2igdDg2 Response to Dr Margaret McCartney's "seams of multiple misinformation" pervading the scientific world - "Evidence in a post-truth world". BMJ 2016; 355: 16363, November 28, 2016.

40 LORD JESUS CHRIST: To the Samaritan woman at the well: "GOD is a Spirit; and they that worship Him, must worship Him in spirit and in truth." Gospel of John .chapter 4 verse 24.

41 Lloyd-Jones DM. 'Spiritual Depression: Its Causes and Cure' Amazon Book Store www.amazon.co.uk >Spiritual-De ISBN 9780802813879 [One of top 100 Millennium Books]

42 Konotey-Ahulu FID. The spiritual and the psychological in Clinical Medicine. Personal View) BMJ 1977; 1:1595 doi:10,1136/6076/1595 June 15 "There is a vast area of man's experience called the spiritual realm which neither Freudian psychoanalysis nor the scientific method can fathom ... Approaches to scientific truth and spiritual truth are different. One scientist will read Dr Lloyd-Jones' 'Spiritual Depression: Its Causes and Cure' (reference 41 above) with much profit while another, with the same qualifications, will find it unintelligible." www.bmj.com/cgi/reprint/1/6076/1595.pdf

43 Lloyd-Jones DM. Conversions Psychological and Spiritual. (Critique of Dr William Sargent's 'Battle for the Mind') https://www.amazon.co.uk >uk 9780851100098 December 1 1959.

44 LORD JESUS CHRIST. For I am not come to call the righteous, but sinners to repentance. Matthew's Gospel chapter 9 verse 13. [Reading of which at about 8pm 24 October 1952 alone in my university rooms in Legon, Ghana, seemed to switch on spiritual eyes that changed me for good]

45 Barker Peter, Boadi-Siaw Samuel. 'Changed by the WORD – The Story of Scripture Union in Ghana.' Scripture Union Ghana, P O Box AN 7388, Accra-North, Ghana. ISBN 9964-87-800-1 "Felix will never be the same again" - p. 18.

46 Metaxas Eric. 'BONHOEFFER – Pastor, Martyr, Prophet, Spy', Thomas Nelson USA, August 2011 (626 pages).

47 Metaxas Eric. 'AMAZING GRACE. Biography of William Wilberforce'. Authentic Media, USA. October 2013 (344 pages).

48 Metaxas Eric. ‘MARTIN LUTHER: The Man Who Rediscovered GOD and Changed the World’. Viking Press, USA. October 2017 (416 pages).

Competing interests: Competing interest: Believer in The Lord Jesus Christ [Nuntsɔ Yesu Kristo]
https://bit.ly/cRrZ0s

TIME WAS CREATED

Millennium Hymn

with Music by
Dr Felix I D Konotey-Ahulu
https://bit.ly/cRrZ0s

MILLENNIUM HYMN

[Tune: All Time Pre – and Post 2000]

©Felix I D Konotey-Ahulu: Melody and verse 1, 1999:
verses 2 to 7, AD 2000
Harmonised by sister Edna Soyannwo

1

TIME was created, and initiated, by HIM;
Present Time is maintained, accurately, by HIM;
Future Time will be commanded, and held, by HIM
Who, though God, became incarnate at Bethlehem.

2

Now when the fullness of the time was really come,
God sent forth His Son to be born-down-here on earth,
To redeem His people from the curse of sin and death,
Hence His presence in the stable in Bethlehem.

3

Forty times in John's Gospel The Lord said He was sent;
Was sent by God The Father, was sent, He was sent
On a rescue mission; He was sent, He was sent;
So He humbly came to be born in Bethlehem.

4

GOD gave His only Son to pay the price of sin;
The Just for the unjust was killed at Golgotha;
This good news of redemption is just as true today,
AS when angels led the shepherds to Bethlehem.

5

Up from the dead My Sovereign Lord was raised
with might;
He sent THE HOLY SPIRIT to give me His new light,
And to make me glorify His Name, and worship Him,
Like the wise men who adored Him in Bethlehem.

6

One day My Lord in triumph will come again,
When earthly time will cease, and eternity begin;
"Oh how great! How marvellous" will be my
glorious hymn,
When He comes to reign Who first came to Bethlehem.

7

JEHOVAH! IMMANUEL! LORD JESUS CHRIST!
Creator! God with us! Saviour! High Priest!
This amazing, awesome Name, the Name above all names
Explains His miraculous birth in Bethlehem.

Tonic SolFa

d: d r m m d d r r d t d:-

s$_{|}$ m: m f s: m d l l s fe s:-

l l t s d$^{|}$ d$^{|}$ d$_{|}$ d$_{|}$ l: s f m:-

r m f s l t d$^{|}$ r$^{|}$ m$^{|}$: r$^{|}$ r$^{|}$ d$^{|}$:-

mf
Time was cr - ea - ted and i - ni - tia - ted by Him: Pre -
5
sent Time is main - tained a - ccu - rate - ly by Him:
9
Fu - ture Time will be com - mand-ded and held, by Him
f
13
Who though God be - came in - car - nate at Be - thle - hem.
rit.
cresc.